T0130028

# The Truth About You

## A Collection of Poems

DAMION J. CHANDLER

authorHOUSE®

AuthorHouse™
1663 Liberty Drive
Bloomington, IN 47403
www.authorhouse.com
Phone: 1 (800) 839-8640

Published by AuthorHouse  04/30/2018

ISBN: 978-1-5462-3963-5 (sc)
ISBN: 978-1-5462-3962-8 (e)

Print information available on the last page.

This book is printed on acid-free paper.

# Contents

# Bonus Poems

# Under Construction

I really thought I had it all together
I thought my life was cool
But it slowly fell
As quickly as I
Built it
Then came the truth
I didn't have everything
I thought I did
And everything I had
Wasn't promising
And I'm not taking about
Love
I'm talking career wise
And academically
A lot of the problems
That I thought I had with everybody
Else
It was just a cover up
To try and not to deal with the issues I had with myself
But now I'm attentive and daring
Giving myself
Just a little self awareness
Without any interruptions
To finally say
Im under construction
That old me and my old ways
I had to lose
To be rebuilt and repaired
Into something brand new
I'm working on myself
I don't need no one else
To help me find the clues

Of rectifying me
Losing all of those insecurities
I didn't know how love
But I thought I was the best
But now I see
I needed to give my heart a rest
Clear my mind
And get some things off my chest
To finally admit
I'm under construction
Shoveling out all my
Dirty consumptions
I need a fresh start
Right now I'm mending
My peace of mind
And revivifying my heart
So I can be
A fresh new me
Soulful and free
Then rose-fully I can bloom
Im under construction
There's a new me coming soon

# Peter Pan

I was a rebel without a cause
Making fart noises
Writing on the walls
Just a hard headed boy
Pretending to be a super hero
But now my childhood
Seems like such a blur
Because things that aren't supposed to happen
Are starting to occur
I just want to ride my bike
Play outside all night
Until I see the streetlight
But when I look into the mirror
It kind of scares me
Too see a growing mustache
A sprouting beard
And to hear a voice that's deep
Just a couple of years ago, that wasn't me
My mama told me I needed to grow up
And ill admit when she'd spit those words
I was ready to throw up
To be honest the good ole days
I deeply miss
Oh how I wanted to just stay a kid
But my calves are getting thicker
My hands are get bigger
And reality is starting to hit
Life moves on over time
And it's going to keep going
Whether you're rotten or ripe
And I didn't want to get left behind
So this transformation I had to embrace

But I was so reluctant to the change
My way of thinking is mature
Now I'm a lot sure of my actions
Choosing when to say things
And when they happen
Ill be the first to tell you
I didn't want to grow up
But it was something I had to do
I noticed myself making careful decisions
Now then a couple of years ago
I didn't care what I'd choose
I was a boy whose now a man
I guess ill never be Peter Pan

# *What I Need*

You're always complaining
About what you want and what you need
What about what I need?
Ill break it down for you
Please take heed:
Can I get some compassion?
Some communication?
Cause it seems as though
You can't talk to me and you've
Made it very blatant
What about some intimacy
Rub my cheek
Hold my hand
And what happened to romance?
I wouldn't mind an ounce of respect
And some companionship,
Would that be too much to ask?
It's the little things like this
That make a relationship last
Understand that I got you
For better and for worse
And to throw in a thank you
Every now and then wouldn't hurt
When I'm down and distraught
I need you to be there
Tell me it'll be okay
When I'm feeling tense
Give me a massage
Ask me how was my day
I want to be happy
With you and have fun
And if this is not your idea of a relationship

Then you don't need to be in one
Can I trust you?
Where do your loyalties lie?
Because if I mess up this one time
My heart is on the line
I can't risk that pain
I love you and I can't conceal it
So I'm asking you to give me all these things
Simply because one day when you tell me you love me
I want to feel it.

# Blow Them Away

I have a lot of so called friends
That goes behind my back and hate
Then the next day
They're all in my face
But I don't retaliate
I just blow them away
I must be famous
To have a lot of people
Spit on my name
But I don't worry
I just blow them away
Why should I keep them around?
When they only strive to knock me down
They try to turn my sunshine into rain
But just like wind
I blow them away
With a couple people
I've had quarrels and strife
But there's a reason why
They're not in my life
I'll keep rising to the top
I'll give it my all
It's always the jealous friends
Who say they want me to rise
But secretly waiting for me to fall
But they'll never see me drop
I'll keep a smile on my face
Cause like mosquitoes swarming around me
I just blow them away

# The Way You Love Me

I can't even breathe
I can't even speak
You stole the words
Out of my mouth
Like a devious thief
Like the drummer of my heart
You never skipped a beat
And that's why I love you
because even underneath
The pain and the grief
You still have the energy to love me
Even through all my mischief
You take all my flaws
And turn them into perfection
I can survive outside in this
Lonely world
Knowing that I have your hearts protection
To come home to your charm
Cuddle up in your arms
And giving me endless affection
And this thing called love happened
To me
It seemed so strange
Cause at first I didn't believe
When you've endured so much pain
It gets harder to see
That someone can come along
At any moment
And love you beyond
What you'd dream
And that's exactly what you did
With every touch

And every kiss
I was trapped in your presence
And locked in your embrace
I didn't want to be set free
Because it's not
Why or when
But its the way you love me!

# Against All Odds

I think we all go through a season
Of finding love at the wrong time
But you gave me all the reasons
To keep it going
Instead of letting it die
There were moments when you got mad
There were nights that I cried
But we got together based on defiance
So our feelings we had to sit aside
Yes it awkward at first
You made me laugh
Despite my hurt
Everyone told me don't do it
They said don't give you a chance
But the love you gave
I didn't want to lose it
So they really couldn't understand
Cause all the pain that I had
You'd kill it
Every drop
Even when you didn't know
Somehow you made it stop
Sometimes loving you was kind of like a job
And there were days where I didn't
Want to punch the clock
But just as much bad
We also had the good
I would relive it all again even if I could
So weather you with me or your not
I still remember us in love
We went against all odds
They were betting that we're not going make it

11

Hand shaking on such cruel deals
Some even thought that what were faking
But we didn't owe them no explanation
On what we think is real
They're just mad
Cause they don't have
What we have
Chasing after love after love
But watch us making is last
Some thought that we wasn't fit for each other
Some thought we were moving to fast
With every successful love
There comes a pack of enemies
But I never let their opinions get the best of us
I didn't let it hinder me
You're like my muse
I fed off your energy
We didn't let them end us
We didn't let them call the shots
We loved each other
And we went against all odds

# Come To Me Naturally

Bare all your necessities
Come to me as you are
Let me stimulate your mind
Then eventually your heart
Let me see
What lies beneath
As I peel you apart
Piece by piece
Reveal what you've been
Keeping in the dark
Let me shine on you
Spread all of my light
If i give you my wings
Will you take flight
Here we are face to face
Showing me naked
You came and stole what you wanted
I was here for the taking
As the light flickers
Its shows a shadow of pictures
Us
Untamed and unfiltered
As I glisten in your glitter
I could choose to be anywhere
I wanted to be
But in your arms
Comes no harm
So I slumber comfortably
Together
Intwined
In time
What we thought is just fun

Really made us one
But some define
It as a crime
But rules were made to be broken
And I feel a love unfolding
So let's soak in each other
No words need to be spoken
Just listen to your breath
And it'll tell me all
You've been withholding
So deep within
All under your skin
Imagine how'd I'd feel
With just one kiss
Take me into you
Exhale my love
Make your skin golden
With just the slightest touch
Run to me
Showcase your flaws
You yelled for acceptance
And I heard your call
Without knowing
Your heart so pure
It captured it me....
So I ask you
Can I unmask you
And come to me
Naturally...

# When A Heart Dies

When a Heart dies
I begins to ache
It decreases in size
Then it starts to break
It cries over and over again
This is a heart that can't be mended
Love runs out the department to spare
It just a tiny heart with nothing to share
It won't go into the future
But dwells in the past
Sadly this Is a heart
Thats not going to last
All of a sudden
The heart shuts down
And at the bottom of your chest
You hear a shrill echoing sound
But of course it the redundant cry
This is when a heart dies
Finally the weeping stops
And the tears still shed
Now we know for sure
The heart is dead

# Take It Slow

No I don't know
Your intentions
But you sure got my attention
I stop talking and I listen
To all that you got to say
And whatever you fail to mention
Im sure I won't be missing
Not one thing
Lying next to you
Barely touching
But our elbows are rubbing
And I'm scared to make the next move
So lets take it slow
And wherever we go
I will know that is real
No point in going fast
Cause once we go there
It isn't any turning back
And were liable to crash
So lets just the facts
That wherever this goes
We just need to take it slow
There is nothing wrong
With being cautious
Especially of we're dating
Things may go awry
If we're not patient
So thats why I haven't kissed you
Or even text you that I missed you
Cause every little thing
Could be way more than it seems
So lets take it slow

For one another
Take our time and really get to know
Each other
If we go all the way
Then some things might change
That we won't be ready for
With us at the blame
Why make it harder
If we can survive without the pain
We can hold hands
We can even dance
But as for taking off my pants
Id rather be romanced
Id hope you understand
What I'm trying to say
We have all the time in
the world so lets take it
Day by day
So when I feel what I feel
Believe me you'll know
But up until that moment
Lets just take it slow

# The Break-Up Song

First we begin to argue,
Then we begin fighting
It's a moment of silence
Then were both back to trying
All we hear is this familiar song
And its been playing way to long
I don't know what we did wrong
Or how do we get back on the track
We were once on?
Were stuck in limbo
While the melody is chiming
Love is at the top of the hill
And we just can't climb it
Just listen to the words
Its been playing way to long
I feared to hear this break up song
It's all the same thing
Fussing, yelling, cussing
Not really having a discussion
Instead of love were just fronting
So all that wasted time was for nothing
And I'm sorry to you
Sorry to you heart
We should've never came to this part
How many times have we heard half of the lyrics?
"I'm tired of you"
"I can't do this any more"
But we never finish
When you argue so much
For so long
It's not really an argument, more like a song
The same thing every single time

To the chorus, from the beat
To its heart breaking rhymes
But I don't want to sing it anymore
And I rather not listen
We fell apart because we didn't pay attention
To all that was disappearing
But I guess if we never had it,
There's no way we can miss it

# Save A Hug For You

I know that you've been feeling
That you've had it mighty rough
Life has put you in a game
You're worried you can't keep up
But I am here to say.
That I am here to stay
Through whatever you're going through
It doesn't matter the time
In the day or the night
If you call
I'll run to you
When you come to me
Tired and dreary
Whenever you need it
If you get lost
And hope to seek it.
I'll spread my undying love for you
I'm here with open arms
And I've saved a hug for you

# Thank You

For the way you raised me
For all the times you saved me
Even when I was acting up
And misbehaving
For the tears you dried
And the pain you subsided
Did I ever say thank you
Cause if I never said thank you
I'm telling you now thank you
For all the times you came running
When I was wrong or right
For all the times I was in the dark
Somehow you'd remember to cut on the light
I'm just a reflection of your strength
A mere silhouette of your power
You planted a seed
And so on it
Thrives and grows
From the love I devoured
For all the memories
You bestowed upon me
And I even I had
To learn the hard way
About your life's lessons
But I don't think you quite understand
You are the greatest blessing
And that's just a tiny confession
Of the truth
For they way you protected me
From life's judgment
You'd knew someday they'd give
Now I stand proud and firm

Raised by your hands and cunning wit
For everything you've done
And continue to do
Did I ever say thank you?
Cause if I never said thank you
I'm saying now
Thank you

# *Text Message*

1 text
2 text
And then no reply
3 hours
4 hours
I'm calling it a night
Sleeping it away
With my phone on vibrate
Hoping that you'd call
With a good reason to explain
The gap between messages
Its the only time we talk
So why are you hesitant
And all you got to do is text me back
Reassure me that everything is in tact
I know that your busy
Probably not alone
But when you get some down time
Why don't you check your phone
I'm there
In the notifications list
Are you really preoccupied
Or ignoring the call that
I know you seen you've missed
1 time
2 times
You're on the verge of being dismissed
3 texts
4 texts
I'm about to call it quits
I don't text you
For me not to get a reply

Then you text me In the morning
With some story
About what happened last night
I know you seen my message
Even I if you didn't read it
Well...
Push 1 button
2 buttons
Now your number is deleted.

# Sweet Addiction

In the beginning
Everybody had the feeling
That you were no good for me
But I did what you wanted
I never did listen
To their fact filled opinions
And we've gone crazy
Something went off
When I seen your face
You decided to run
And I decided to chase
Not knowing what i was
Running too
my mistake
So maybe you're dangerous
You live a loaded life
But when you fall in love
There's no need to think it twice
You had me breathless
Almost going psychotic
So strong
Like Gin seducing an alcoholic
Our love was a fire
Fueled by feelings and friction
And I'd run back to you every time
Just like an addiction
My fixation
I couldn't shake you off
Did whatever you wanted
When you wanted
No matter what the cost
We were free and careless

So out if control
They hated me for loving you
But it didn't stop the show
Taking over the world
That was the goal
But before we could get there
Troubles started to unfold
I was getting weak and weary
I couldn't hang on any more
Years of torment
And unforgotten pain
I guess its safe to say
I lost the most dangerous game
It was poisonous
Killing really fast
We loved each other
Until the last crash
Even after the flames
And all the suffering
I'll always feels like something
Is missing
Your love was my drug
The most sweetest addiction

# Broke

It's official
I'm bankrupt
I can't buy no more
Of your love
I'm barely down to dimes
And pennies
My funds are deadly insufficient
It's too high
Too expensive
To keep buying your love
When it makes no difference
My checks are starting to bounce
I'm on my last twenty
I guess I'll put my heart on law-away
Cause I can't afford
Another heartbreak
I went broke trying to love you
I didn't even have spare change
To buy away the pain
My heart is in overdraft
My wallet is empty
Now i know it's no refunds
But I guess that's what I get
For being so willing
To spend every dime
When all I really wanted
Was an ounce of your time
I'm so broke
No cash
My credit cards are declined
It's crazy that I had to pay
When you gave it to others

For free
At least I kept all my receipts
My funds are deadly insufficient
Your love is too high
Too expensive
And not even worth
All that I'm giving

# Safest Place

In a room
Dark and deep
Big and strong
But quietly beats
Nobody here
Just you in me
All alone....in peace
You saw me scared
And drowning in fear
Then you grabbed me by the hand
And brought me here
I believe the safest place
For me to start
Is your heart
To touch you
And get to know you
To love you and show you
That I won't disappear
Outside it's foreign and strange
That's why I would rather stay
In the depths of you
Where it's safe
I am no superhero
But only in your embrace
That's why I believe
For me, inside your heart
Is the safest place.

# Pack Of Wolves

We thrive in a cold world
So what do you expect
Frostbite from my mouth
Now your words
You regret
I come from a line of survivors
The scars to prove it too
They're the backbone of my strength
And the voice of my truth
They're not something to be toyed with
No common mammal
Will go against them
Reminiscent to wolf
We travel in a pack
Together
Through whatever
They loyalty remains
In tact
My sister
My stepdad
My 2 brothers
And my mother
They stand before and behind me
Like no other
The mind of a beast
Thick skin
With blood on their teeth
Anyone who causes harm
They'll hunt you
Then feast
I've seen they're claws
Ripping what's in their way

I've seen they're fangs
Tearing apart disloyal prey
We step out on our paws
Silent so you can't hear
But If one attacks
They all attack
If You bite first
Then they'll bite back
With a snap of a finger
They'll eat you for food
We hold hands
We pray
Probably howl to the moon
Here's a family you don't want to cross
And I've came across a lot of fools
But then again only a fool
Would go against
A pack of wolves

# Clueless

They all kept saying
You were arrogant
And its plainly evident
That thats not my preference
You were risk taking and daring
Slick mouth and uncaring
And I didn't want to put myself through
Something that would later be irrelevant
But the more you came around
The crazier this sounds
And it even got hectic
Cause I couldn't stay away
And it was an open case
For me to figure out
What was making this attraction
So magnetic
There was plenty of times
When I said I didn't want you before
But as quiet as kept
That made me want you more
Im not really sure
But I'm going to explore
Why you make my heart love you
Beyond its core
And since then
Ive been wanting to
Talk to you longer
Touch you deeper
Love you stronger
To know that I got to keep you
I don't want to say I need you
Because I secretly bleed you

Oh yes its a mystery
On how we have this chemistry
Cause it was to hard to believe
That even without a history
That this was meant to be
Maybe so
Maybe not
But you were meant for me
I cant fathom to deny it
Although I've tried it
I even tried to act undecided
But like I said it was all an act
And I guess its a well known fact
That opposites attract

# Guardian Of Your Heart

I'm just the guy
from years ago
That found your heart
And brought it home
You set out
Alone and own your own
But you figured out
When it's gone
Its gone
So I heard your heart is lost again
I'll volunteer to find it
Wherever it is
No matter how far the trip
I don't mind it
That wave
I'll ride it
Because you given me
Everything
Even things that I never asked for
So I'll be that everything you need
Because thats what you asked for
I'll stand strong and brave
No one will harm you
Until my name is on a grave
Like I promised you
To be the guardian of You heart
Slay every demon
Thats giving me a reason
To play my part
Every captor
Every threat
That comes near

shall meet death
Even after the war is over
And the blood is all spilled
You'll find me in the corner of you soul
Its where I call home
A place I've built
So I will deflect
All negativity
And protect this vicinity
All though many have tried to hinder
Me
We all have our hero's
So let me be yours
Let my love spill on you
Until I can't pour no more
I gave an oath
A promise, to be that light
In the dark
Yes, without any hesitation
I'll be the guardian of your heart.

# Sleeping With The Enemy

4am
I hear you wake suddenly
I lay there motionless
But you think I'm asleep
I feel the covers drag off
And the wood planking
To your feet
A whisper
Then a zipper
Shoes
Your jacket
Now the rustling of your keys
Unlock the door
And you leave
No goodbye
Not even a rose on my pillow
To thank me for my services
You go back to your life
While I'm stained for life
I guess I encouraged this
If I say love you
Technically I'm in the wrong
Because there's someone other
Another lover
Who loves you when you there
Or even when you're gone
That kind of love
I can't compete
Am I just someone
Of the many ones
Who you lay down
And take to sleep

But you're not my lover
Not my friend
But the enemy
If I keep on with this
It will be end of me
How many more times
Must I fight back the tears
Risk the risk
Get a grip
And text you
To tell you I need you here
But that's not what I'm supposed
To do
My role is just staying silent
Speak when spoken too
You claim you got to text me first
Then I can reply back to you
I kind of get the understanding
But some parts has me confused
Is this "you don't call me,
I'll call you?"
This is what I get
Because we tend to forget
That just because you're loving me
Doesn't mean you love me
You're not my crush
Just somebody I spend my day with
You're not my friend
Just someone I lay with
This is the kind of love
That will hinder me
But what more could I expect
From sleeping with the enemy

# The Beautiful Ones

Like a star glowing
Through the night
Faster than a speed of light
The ones who
Everybody loves
And wants to be
You're full happiness
With just a mere taste
Of their presence
The atmosphere
Of angels with an aroma
From heaven
They're the beautiful ones
Who do beautiful things
Like dry some ones tears
Release an unforgivable pain
Or heal a heart break
The ones who saves the day
When your down
And they make you feel okay
The people that run
To the rescue when no
One else comes
For they are the beautiful ones
Just ordinary people
Living their lives
But unknowingly saving another's
One at time
Always so polite
With a sun ray for a smile
The ones who you'd want around for a while
Be careful how you treat people

One day you might need them
Its free to be nice
And you don't have to have a reason
They're around you
They surround you
Your friends
The family you love
That's who they are
The beautiful ones

# Lonely Tonight

When you're far
And your heart
Yearns to be near
I'm just a text
Or call away from
Riding all your fears
But if you need just a little more
Affection
Then I'm heading in that direction
Cause you don't have to be lonely tonight
I'll come in the mid of the night
And I'll stay by your side
Giving you all my warmth
I'm on my way
Talking to you
Pulling out my driveway
Cause I don't want to be lonely tonight
And you and only you can make it right
Windows down
Smooth ride
Did you get my text?
I'm outside
You see the gleam of my headlights
You don't ever have to worry about needing me
Cause by your side is where I choose to be
I signed up for this
So that means I'll take it all
The late night vists
And the early morning phone calls
You don't ever have to be lonely So when you need me just
Roll over and hold me

# I'll Be There For You

You've proven your loyalty to me
There's no need to question
Your trust
So I promise to be there
When things get a little rough
It's nothing you wouldn't do for me
Everything I ask for you provide
So whatever it is that you need
It's no lie, that I'm going to supply
Cause you held the umbrella
When I was in a storm
Pulled me close in ya arms
Kept me safe and warm
So ill be here for you
When you win or lose
Whatever they throw at us
We'll get through
In sunshine
Or in rain
I'll be there
When your full of joy
Or when your overwhelmed
With pain
So don't worry about
What to do
I got it
You took care of me
So I'll be there for you
All I want to see is your smile
But I have no problem drying your tears
When your scared
Just call on me

I'll kill your fears
See its only fair
That I take care of you
Cause when I was alone
Confused and crying
You loaned me comfort
And took me out of hiding
You've shown your love
That's a true fact
So now it's time
To pay you back
Through the ups and downs
The lies and truth
You can count on me
To be here for you
For better or for worse
When its good or when it hurts
I'll be the one you'll need
Whatever you need me to do
When you need saving
Im coming the rescue.
No matter how many times
I say thank you
It still won't be enough
You bend over backwards
trying to make me happy
So supporting you is a must
Whenever you're in need
Just call on me I want be far.
You healed my heart
And i didn't ask you too.
You took care of me
So its only fair that
I'll be there for you

# *Stupid*

I'm stupid
I'm an idiot
I should've seen it coming
You always did
What you do to me
Which was a lie
Cause you were just using me
And like a dummy
I fell for it
Your hugs and kisses
Must've weaken my defenses
Because no matter what I said
It didn't make a difference
How you had me influenced
From your lustful limericks
Maybe I was in denial
And needed something to
Hold on to
You said to me
Everything thing
You heart told you too
And stupid enough
I am the dunce
Because I believed you
Why do I always fall in love
With the ones who
Isn't ready love
Say that they're willing
But only ending up giving not
Enough
I'm tired of trying to chase you
Playing catch up isn't no fun

Maybe you thought it was a game
To hide and then seek me
With so much pain
You never wanted to be here
So I knew eventually you'd run
Scared of what I could do
Maybe scared of what we could pursue
Set a goal
Build a dynasty
Make our dreams come true
But I guess that was too hard
And it was even harder to win your heart
I guess I played myself from the start.
Cause I'm the only one in the dark
I was foolish
Oh why did I do it
I already had doubts to
Conclude it
I always fall in love
With the ones who aren't ready to love
How could I be so stupid.

# Deep Under Water

If you think nobody is on your side
Well I am
And if you think nobody understands
What you're going through
I understand
You don't have to be shy
When it comes to me
Just unlock your heart
Let me hold the key
I know that this is scary
And weird to you
Going into a whole new world
Will have you terrified and confused
But it's something you must go through
No one said you had to do it
On your own
So don't ever think
You're all alone
You're so deep under water
And it's only going to get harder
The more you try
To deny who you are
Swim to the surface
Your going deeper
To the ground
The more you lie to yourself
You're going to drown
I'm going to reach out my hand
Bring you to the shore
And I recognize the signs
Cause I've been here before
This isn't a dream

This isn't a daze
And I can only help you
If you're willing to be saved
I know your fear they're going to leave
And reject you like everybody else
But the only way to float to the coast line
Is too start trusting yourself
You're too deep under water
I can barely see you
Don't give out
Don't you dare drown
There are people who still need you
Just open up to me
Let the worry drain from your heart
I'll try to save you
But I'm no lifeguard
Warmer you get
Hotter and hotter
Please don't drown in everybody's thoughts
You're too deep under water

# Sorry Apology

Oh darling
I never knew you
Cared so much
Your pride was in the way
To admit
You've missed my touch
But I guess you've been
Doing some thinking
I guess you've stop drinking
And finally came to your senses
And now you're here to to say "I'm sorry"
Saying you never wanted to hurt me
It's back in the past
And all has been forgiven and forgotten
But I wish it was that easy
To take you back
Like you never broke my heart
You even stepped on the shards
You left screaming
Yelling and confused
Didn't give me a chance to explain
My point of view
If I knew you was going to act that way
In would've never put my opinion
In it
But what more could I expect
Because it was your world and I was just living in it
Now months has flown by
Haven't heard one word from you
And randomly you show up
Wanting to have a word or two
I have nothing to say

Or nothing to prove
I'm not the one who
Gave the fire the fuel
But yet here you are
Needing to start over
Saying you've changed
Your transition may be in effect
But the pain still remains
You gave me the deepest crack
You could give a glass heart
And that's just pure honesty
But your remedy
For fixing the pieces
Is some tape
And a sorry apology..?

# Ugly

You know it's not good
To believe everything you hear
People blame you
Shame you
Ridicule and name you
Until their lies become your fear
But you're breaking
Your own heart
By picking yourself apart
You look into the mirror
And you don't like what you see
And you think you're ugly
So you change what you wear
You dye your hair
To seem beautiful to someone else, not valuing yourself
That's ugly
Criticizing the very things
That make you you
Pretending to be someone you're not
Not facing the truth
It's been some time
Since you said you loved yourself
You say that you're fine
When you want to scream for help
We can't see the real you
If you portray somebody else
But no one ever asks
So you never tell
But you are the pillar
To your own meaning of
Beautiful
It's written all over your face

The pieces of you
No they can't be replace
It's a work of art
How god created you from
His hands
So every thing you deny
It was all apart of his plan
You think you're ugly?
Well look into the mirror
And chant "I love me"
Because believing in you insecurities
And picking yourself apart
That's ugly

# *This Is 24*

As I look back,
On all the years,
Of becoming me
Now a new story begins
As I close the chapter to 23
I've grown
I've taken blow after blow
But somehow in the midst of all the darkness
I still glow
Im stepping outside myself
Where no man chooses to dwell
Realizing how much I've evolved
From the last March 12th
Although they tried to stumble me
I didn't let them crumble me.
Yes a few fumbled me
But stayed grounded
And became a humble me
Because the most important goal
Was unconditionally loving me!
Of course they try to block me
And at times hinder me
Days I'd look into the mirror
And realize that sometimes
I was my own worst enemy
But with growth comes change
Whats a sun to shine
With no rain?
So you see?
It hasn't been easy
All the late night cries
To me telling myself its going to be alright

Through every calamity
By the grace of god
My friends
And my family
I'm still here surviving in
World they said I didn't "fit in"
But the plan was never to blend
But to stand out
Own my mistakes
While I'm drenched in sin
That old me
Yeah...he's ran his course
So this is the me I've been waiting for
To burst out of that shell
Sprout out of that cocoon
And spray the world with my galore
Another year for me
And aren't I glad to be here
Hand on the knob
As I open yet another door
For 23 has came and gone
This is 24.

# Life x 25

Wake up
It's time
A quarter of a century
Gone down the line
The 5th year in my 20s
My has it been a ride
The ups and downs
Being lost
To being found
The pain and the joy
Through the silence
And the the noise
I still remain
Here
With the rewards that I worked for
And with every reward comes a whiff
Of motivation to work more
To do more
To be more
And here and now
I rip off the skin
That belonged
To the age 24
I'm happy
Peacefully sublime
It's definitely true
When they say
Things get better with time
All the positive energy I wade through
I want it to multiply
Sending a rush of encouragement
And serene vibes

Live it how you want it
Respect it, and own it
Get a chance
Take a shot
Don't blow it
This is my destiny
I chose it
I've made up my mind
The door to 24 is closed
I can hear bells chimes
Because now
This is
MY life times 25.

Printed in the United States
by Bookmasters

Printed in the United States
By Bookmasters